STUDIES
IN HISTORY AND
GEOGRAPHY

People and Places

Rosemary Rees

Janet Withersby

Heinemann

First published in Great Britain by Heinemann Library, Halley Court, Jordan Hill, Oxford OX2 8EJ
a division of Reed Educational and Professional Publishing Ltd

OXFORD FLORENCE PRAGUE MADRID ATHENS MELBOURNE AUCKLAND KUALA LUMPUR
SINGAPORE TOKYO IBADAN NAIROBI KAMPALA JOHANNESBURG GABORONE
PORTSMOUTH NH CHICAGO MEXICO CITY SAO PAULO

Designed by Aricot Vert Design

Illustrations by Sally Damant

Printed in the UK by Jarrold Book Printing Ltd, Thetford

00 99 98 97 96

10 9 8 7 6 5 4 3 2 1

ISBN 0 431 07899 8

This title is also available in a hardback library edition (ISBN 0 431 07890 4).

British Library Cataloguing in Publication Data

Rees, Rosemary, 1942 –
  People and places – (Local studies in history and geography)
  1. Geography – Juvenile literature
  I. Title II. Withersby, Janet
  910

Acknowledgements

The Publishers would like to thank the following for permission to reproduce photographs:
ACE Photo Agency: p.17; Allan Cash: p.11; Mary Evans Picture Library: p,24;
Honeywell: p.8; National Railway Museum: p.12; Ordnance Survey: pp.5, 10, 21;
Roger Scruton: pp.3, 4, 6, 7, 20, 22-25, 27-29; Sealand: pp.13, 26; Skyscan Balloon Photography: p.9

Cover photograph reproduced with permission of Zentrale Farbbild Agentur GmbH

Maps reproduced from Ordnance Survey mapping with the permission of The Controller
of Her Majesty's Stationery Office © Crown Copyright, Licence No. MC8575 OM.

Our thanks to Jane Shuter for her comments in the preparation of this book.

Every effort has been made to contact copyright holders of any material reproduced in this book.
Any omissions will be rectified in subsequent printings if notice is given to the Publisher.

Contents

Looking at places

Places are different

Where are you? What is the name of the place you are in? What is it like? Look out of your window. What can you see? Think about the other places you know. Every place is different and every place has its own story.

Looking around us

If you look out of your window you might see some hills or sloping land, or perhaps the land is flat. You might see water, open spaces or buildings.

You can find out more about the place you are in by looking at it very carefully. You might think of reasons why there are buildings or open spaces. You might discover which are the oldest buildings. This could help you to find out which jobs people have been doing here for a long time and which jobs are new.

This is a photograph of a village called Hornby. It is beside a place where it was safe to cross the river. Roads met at this river crossing and people met there too. Many people came to buy and sell at Hornby market. These are the reasons why a village grew up here.

*This is a map which shows us part of a river's route. The River Lune flows past Hornby and other villages in the **valley**. You can see more rivers flowing into the River Lune. They make the river grow wider as it travels to the sea.*

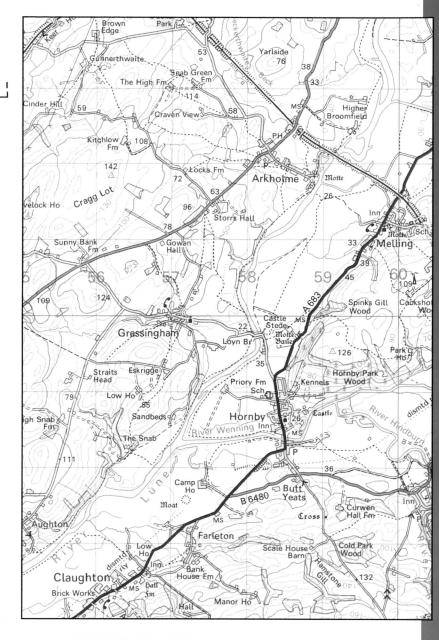

Looking at pictures

People enjoy visiting and exploring different places. They take photographs and buy postcards to help them remember those places. You could draw or take photographs of people and places in your **town** or **village**. Old photographs and pictures of the same place will help you to discover what it was like in the past.

Looking at maps

Have you ever looked down on a place from an aeroplane window? Maps are like drawings made from an aeroplane. On a map you can follow journeys that people make from one place to another. You can follow the routes of rivers as they flow down from the hills to the sea.

LOOK OUT

People need to cross rivers to travel to other places. Look out for ways in which people cross rivers. Is there a river near where you live?

Time detectives

What is this place like?

Rebecca, Jyoti and Mark are looking at a huge photograph of the land and river near Hornby. The photograph was taken from an aeroplane. The children used a map to find the names of the **town** and **villages** on the photograph.

Why do we need place names?

People need to give places names so that they can talk about them. We use place names to tell people where we live and to describe the places we have visited.

Looking for clues about the past

The children used the Finding Out cards to investigate the names of the places on the map. They discovered **Anglo-Saxon** or **Viking** words in all the place names that were on the map.

Rebecca and Jyoti are adding names to places on the photograph.

Finding Out

ANGLO-SAXON WORDS

If Anglo-Saxon people wanted to talk about a group of farms or a village they used one of these two words

(ton) (Hal*ton*) or

(ham) (Peters*ham*)

If Anglo-Saxon people wanted to talk about a place where a leader and his people lived they said the leader's name first and then said

(ing) (Mell*ing* means the place where Mell and his people lived)

Finding Out

VIKING WORDS

If Viking people wanted to talk about a group of farms or a village they used this word

(by) (Grims*by*)

If Viking people wanted to talk about a valley they used this word

(dale) (Allen*dale*)

If Viking people wanted to talk about a church they used this word

(kirk) (*Kirk*by)

If Viking people wanted to talk about a piece of dry ground in a marshy place they used this word

(holme) (Oxen*holme*)

Who gave these places their names?

The names tell us that more than a thousand years ago Anglo-Saxon people had homes in this river **valley**. Later, Viking people came to live here, too. They described their villages in their own languages.

The children worked out that Viking people gave the village of Kirkby Lonsdale its name. It means 'the village with a church in the valley of the River Lune'.

The village called Melling gave the children a clue about Anglo-Saxon times. They worked out that a man called Mell was the leader of the Saxon people who lived in this village.

This photograph shows Dean and Satveer with their map. The yellow labels show places with Anglo-Saxon names. The orange labels point to places with Viking names.

Why did people choose to live here?

Dean and Satveer made a map of the River Lune. They used model houses for the town and villages. They decided that Anglo-Saxon people and Viking people chose to build their villages beside places where it was safe to cross the river.

Growing towns

These photographs were taken in 1996 in the town of Milton Keynes. They show ways people travel to and from the town.

Aylesbury Dunstable (A5)

Milton Keynes North South & West Central Milton Keynes Buckingham A 421 (A 4146)

Woburn Sands A 5130

Newport Pagnell M1 A 5130

GRAND UNION CANAL

Towns are meeting places

Towns are busy places where people meet. They might shop or work there. They might go to school or to places where they enjoy themselves. Lots of people live in towns but some people just visit them. Many journeys begin or end in towns.

How do people travel to towns?

People travel in different ways. How they travel depends on how far they have to go. It also depends on how much money they can spend.

Different towns have different ways in which people can travel. Some towns have railways and buses which link them to other places. They may have **canals** or an airport. Some towns are close to motorways, but people may choose to travel along smaller, quieter roads.

LOOK OUT

Look for different ways people travel to the place you live.

How did towns begin?

Over 2000 years ago, before the Romans came to Britain, people were travelling along roads and tracks to places where they could meet other people. Here they exchanged things they had grown or made for the things they needed. The meeting places became market places.

When did towns grow?

More and more people chose to live and work near market places. Some markets grew into small towns in **Roman** and **Viking** times but most people still lived and worked in **villages**.

In **Victorian** times, factories were built in many small towns. People moved from villages to towns to work in them.

More houses were needed for the people to live in. Some places quickly became large towns. Now, most people live in towns.

Towns by river crossings

Some safe places for travellers to cross rivers became meeting places, market places, and then towns. Place names which have words like 'bridge' and **'ford'** in them tell us that they are by a river crossing. Cambridge, Stratford and Oxford are examples. Do you live in a town or village by a river crossing?

This photograph shows a town called Stratford. There was a ford here where a Roman road crossed the River Avon. You can see that it has grown into a busy town. How do people cross the river today?

Growing ports

What is a harbour?

A harbour is a place where ships shelter from the winds and waves of the high seas. The water is deep enough for ships and boats to be **moored** there, while their **cargoes** are loaded and unloaded. Fishermen can mend their nets and sell their fish. People can sail to foreign countries, and come back again.

What is a port?

A port is a special harbour where large ships from all over the world come to load and unload their cargoes or passengers. A port needs good railway links or good road links with many other towns to bring cargoes and passengers to and from the ships quickly.

Use the map on this page to find out how goods and passengers travel to and from the port of Felixstowe today.

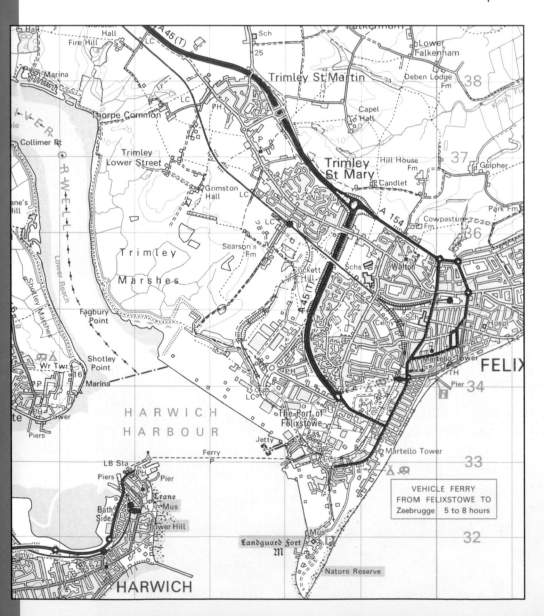

This map shows Felixstowe in Suffolk. Two rivers flow into the sea here. For more than a thousand years ships have sailed up these rivers to find a sheltered place to unload their cargoes. Felixstowe was a good place to build a port.

This is a photograph of the port of Felixstowe in the 1990s. What might happen to Felixstowe if ship-owners start to use another port instead?

How old are ports?

York was a port in **Viking** times. But modern ships need deeper water than Viking ships, so York is no longer a port.

Many new ports were built in **Victorian** times. They were built for larger ships so they had to be nearer to the sea, where the water was deeper.

Steam power

Steam power speeded up work and travel in Victorian times. New steam-powered ships carried cargoes across the sea faster and more reliably than ships powered by the wind and sails. More ships sailed into the ports, and extra docks were needed. Railway lines were built to carry heavy goods quickly from ports to large **towns** and factories.

Who decided to change Felixstowe into a port?

When Queen Victoria became queen in 1837, Felixstowe was a seaside **village**. In the 1870s a businessman called George Tomlin, who had money and good ideas, decided to change this village into a port. A new railway line was built to join the new port to other towns.

How did Felixstowe grow?

Felixstowe became a busy port and seaside town. Extra people were needed to work there, so new families came to live in the town. They needed houses, shops, churches, schools, colleges and parks, and so the town grew.

LOOK OUT

Is there a main road, railway or canal which links a town near you to a port or harbour? How could you find out?

Beside the seaside

How did seaside towns begin?

Long ago, the only places beside the seaside were harbours and small **villages** where fishermen lived with their families. Then, about 250 years ago, a few seaside places were built for wealthy people. These wealthy people went in their **carriages** to places like Brighton to enjoy fresh, sea air.

Why did people go to the seaside?

In Victorian times, **industrial towns** were smoky and dirty. Many people wanted to have fun in the fresh air of the seaside. In the 1840s new railways gave many more people the chance to travel. Some rich businessmen thought many people would use the railways to travel to the seaside. So they built new holiday towns on land beside the sea. Blackpool was one of the places the businessmen chose for a holiday town.

How did seaside towns grow?

Railway lines were built and people came for seaside holidays, or to live and work in the new seaside towns. Blackpool businessmen wanted to attract more visitors to their new seaside town. They had posters put up at railway stations in other towns to persuade people to choose Blackpool for their day-trips and holidays.

This is a railway station poster. It was printed about a hundred years ago. Look at the photograph of modern Blackpool on page 13. Can you see any buildings in modern Blackpool which are about a hundred years old?

LOOK OUT

Look out for posters in modern railway stations. Can you find any that tell you about other places to visit? What do they tell you about those places?

What is this place like now?

The photograph on this page shows part of the seaside town of Blackpool. People come to this place to enjoy themselves. Some come on trains but most people travel in cars or coaches. A motorway has been built to bring traffic all the way to Blackpool. People park their cars in Blackpool's enormous car parks.

Why do people come here?

Visitors come to Blackpool for a day-trip or for a longer holiday. They enjoy the sun, sea and sand, and they need hotels, cafés and shops. They want to visit the funfair, circus, zoo and theatres. The people who work in all these places live in Blackpool to be near their work, or they travel into Blackpool every day.

This modern photograph of Blackpool was taken from an aeroplane. Can you think of any reasons why there were not many people on the beach that day?

Clues from names

What's in a name?

Have you ever wondered how streets, roads and lanes got their names?

Some roads were made when the houses in the road were first built. Names for these roads might have been chosen by the builder who built the houses.

Some road names are very old. They are useful because their names help you to find out about places.

Where do these roads go?

Look at the road name signs in the picture. Banbury Road is in a town called Stratford. It tells you about journeys people make to and from this place. People have been travelling along this road from Stratford to Banbury town for hundreds of years.

The children you see in this book live near Old Lancaster Lane. Most people have forgotten this narrow old way to Lancaster because now there is a wide main road and a motorway to take them there.

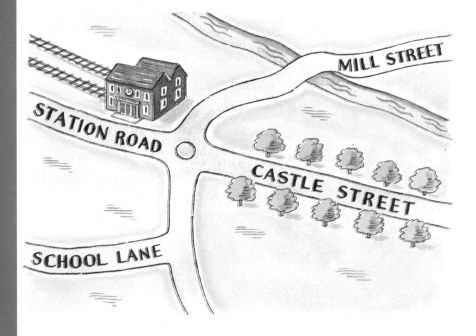

Be a name detective

Some road names tell you how to find your way to special buildings. If the castle in a **town** has been pulled down, a street name, like Castle Street, could help you find out where it used to be.

Royal names

Some children noticed these three road names in their town. They recognized the names. They belonged to Queen Victoria and her family. The children thought that Victoria Street might have been built when Victoria was queen. They made a royal family **time-line** to help them work out when the houses in those roads might have been built.

Ancient ways

Roman Road is the name of a road that does not look very old. The modern road has been built on top of the road that the Romans made.

Days to remember

New houses and streets were being built in towns all over Britain at the time of Queen Victoria's **diamond jubilee** in 1897 and King Edward's **coronation** in 1901. This is the reason why many towns have a Jubilee Terrace and a Coronation Street.

LOOK OUT

Look around you and think about the road names you can see. Perhaps they can help you find out about the place where you live.

A different landscape

Do places change?

The map on this page shows part of a **town** which was built in the 1950s. Until the 1950s the **landscape** was quite different and there was only a small **village** here. It was called Kirkby. Now the village has grown into a town, and the land is covered with houses, roads, schools and shops.

The builders of the new town decided to help people to remember what it was like when it was a village. They put clues in the road names.

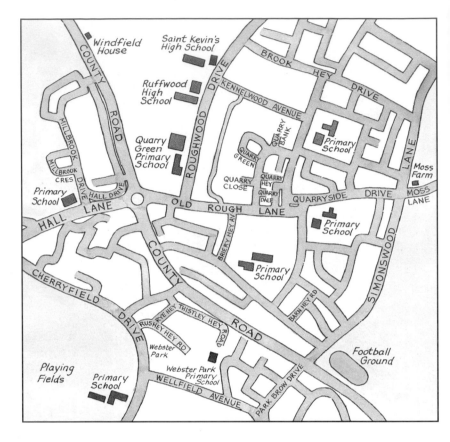

This street map shows part of the new town at Kirkby, near Liverpool.

Clues in Kirkby's road names

Look at the road names on the map. Can you discover what the fields were called? (*Hey* is another word for field.) Were there any woods here?

The old farm houses in the village were built from stone. Can you find the stone **quarry** where the stone came from?

There was a water **mill** near Kirkby Hall where corn was ground into flour. Have the builders left any clues about the mill and the hall in the road names?

LOOK OUT

Look for road names near you which tell you about fields, woods, brooks or farms. What would you find in these places today?

Why do landscapes change?

In **Victorian** times, many more people came to live in towns. New streets of houses were built on the edges of towns. They covered the green countryside.

When did your landscape change?

Look around when you travel into town. Some houses have **datestones** to tell us when they were built. You might be able to spot some datestones on houses built in the 1880s or the 1890s, when Queen Victoria was an old lady. These houses were probably on the edge of the town when they were new. Are they still on the edge of town or has the town grown larger since then?

Are landscapes still changing?

You may know of some houses which are being built near you. If you do, try to remember what the land was used for before the builders came. Do you know why the houses were built? Do you know what your place was like before your house was built?

This is a photograph of a new house which is being built. The builders have just started to put up the walls. What do you think the land was used for before the builders came?

Who lives here?

Do house names tell us about people?

Most houses have numbers, but some houses have names as well. Some families make jokes about their own names when they choose names for their houses. Jane and Robert called their house Janrob. Ann and David Bird and their children called their house The Nest.

Do house names tell us about people at work?

Your doctor might have a sign to show people where the surgery is.

Farm houses usually have signs. The sign for Sandy Lane Farm tells you that Mr Swift and his sons are farmers. They keep mainly cows, and sell their milk to dairies.

Some houses have been made into offices. No one lives there now, but signs will help you to find out about the work people do there.

What do house names tell us about the past?

These pictures of house names were found on buildings in a **village**. All these buildings are now ordinary houses, but their names tell us that they were places where people lived and worked in the past. They tell us about the jobs people used to do in the village.

What happened to the post office?

In the village there is a house called The Old Post Office. Old people in the village remember when this was a busy post office and shop. They bought stamps and groceries there and posted letters and parcels. Then came a time when more people had cars and many people in the village started to travel into **town** for their shopping.

The village post office had to close because it did not have enough customers. Now the old post office has been changed into a family home. The parents in this house work in the town. Can you think of any reasons why the miller, baker, teacher and **blacksmith** don't work in these buildings any more?

LOOK OUT

Do you know how old your school is?
You might be able to discover where the children
went to school before your school was built.

Lost places

Clues about forgotten places

Names can give us clues about forgotten **landscapes**. Some people choose a name for their house which describes the place where the house was built. If a house is near a river it might be called Riverside House.

A name might not seem right now because the place has changed. An old house called Three Trees has only one tree today, but perhaps there were three trees in the garden when the house was new.

Sometimes you need to be a detective

The house in the photograph is a hundred years old. It has a name sign which says 'Park View'. Why do you think it is called Park View? The people who live here now can only see a new school and new houses from their windows. Perhaps when the house was new the family who lived there were able to see a park from the house. Do you think there was a park nearby? Where has the park gone?

*This is the house called Park View. It is in a small **town** called Lytham, near Blackpool.*

PARK VIEW RD.

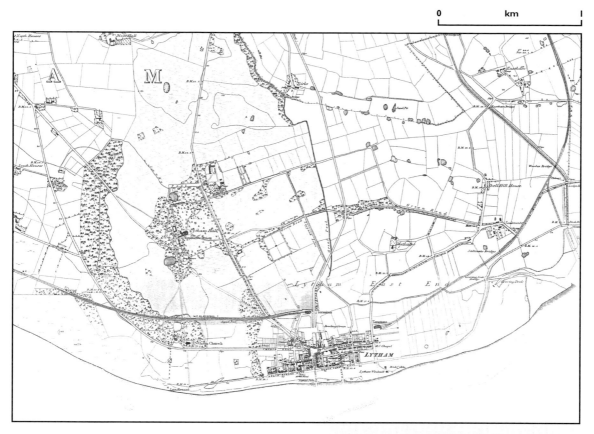

What other clues can you use?

What was this place like 150 years ago? Lytham town was a very small place then. Find Lytham Hall on the map. It was a big house surrounded by a huge park. The park belonged to the rich family who lived at Lytham Hall. Can you find the woods and the open spaces in their park? The first people to live at Park View must have been able to see these woods and grassy spaces when they moved into their new house on the edge of the park.

What happened to the park?

New houses, schools and roads have been built on the south part of the park, near Park View. The people at Park View can now see these new buildings instead of the park.

*This map of Lytham was made in 1844. It was found in Lytham Library. A modern map shows that Lytham Park is much smaller now because Lytham town has grown bigger. You might find old maps of your town or **village** in your local history library.*

LOOK OUT

Look out for any place names near you which do not seem to be right. Perhaps you can find where a lost place has gone.

Clues to the past: pub signs

Investigating pub and inn signs

Many **pubs** and **inns** found in **towns** and **villages** today were built in **Victorian** times. The names on their pub signs were chosen then. Many of these names are still the same today. Looking at pub signs can tell us about people in the past.

Famous names

Have you seen any pub signs named after royal people such as Prince Albert or the Prince of Wales? Some are named after famous leaders like Admiral Lord Nelson or Sir Winston Churchill. You might know pubs which are named after famous battles like Waterloo or Trafalgar, or important inventions like the railway engine called the Rocket. Which modern famous name would you choose for a new pub today? Why?

These are photographs of pub signs. There is a portrait of Sir Winston Churchill and a map of the place where Britain won a famous sea battle at Trafalgar.

Who was important here?

Some pub signs will help you to find out about families who are famous in your area. You might see pub signs with **coats of arms** painted on them. There are also pubs with names like the Derby Arms, or the Percy Arms. These help us to find out the names of rich families who owned some of the land, farms and buildings in your town or village. Sometimes land has belonged to one family for hundreds of years.

How can we find out about them?

Look at the pub sign at the Devonshire Arms Hotel. Is there a local family name like this on a pub sign in your area? This might help you find out more about your place in the past. You could ask questions about this local family and look for answers in the library. You could also look for the family name in an old church nearby. Or you might discover more at the old family home if it is open to visitors.

You may know a pub near you which is called the Duke of Devonshire, the Devonshire Arms or the Cavendish Arms. If you do, you can be sure that the Duke of Devonshire owns or once owned land near you.

This is Chatsworth House, in Derbyshire, where the Cavendish family have lived for 300 years. This family owns land all over England. The head of the family is called the Duke of Devonshire.

LOOK OUT

Look for famous people and events on pub signs. They will help you find out more about the place and its past.

Workers and travellers

Why do we have pubs?

Pubs have always been places where people meet. People go to a pub for something to eat and drink, or to enjoy themselves.

Pub names and people's work

In some places, many people did the same work. Pubs were often named after the groups of workers who drank there. A pub called the **Colliers'** Arms tells you that many people who lived near the pub worked in coal mines.

The **Quarrymen's Inn**, the **Brickmakers'** Arms, the **Ropers'** Inn and the **Glassblower** tell you how local people earned their livings in the past. Why do you think there were large groups of workers doing these jobs in **Victorian** times?

*The person who painted the **blacksmith** on this pub sign might have found out about the blacksmith's work by looking at paintings like this one. It was painted about 160 years ago by an artist called Edward Landseer. Do we still need blacksmiths today?*

BLACKSMITHS ARMS

JOHN SMITH'S

Why do travellers stop at pubs?

Long ago, travel was slow. People on long journeys needed places to eat, drink and warm themselves and perhaps a place to sleep. These are some of the reasons why many pubs are called the Traveller's Rest. Some pubs were named after the sort of travellers who came there.

How did people travel here in the past?

If you look at a pub today you might find that there is a large car park near by. It is possible that old buildings have been pulled down to make space for the car park. Those old buildings probably included stables and perhaps a coach house.

Pub names like the Packhorse Inn, the Carters' Arms or the Coach and Horses give us clues about the sort of people who used the pub in the past. The Railway Tavern and the Station Hotel, or the Ship Inn tell us about the ways many people used to travel there.

Some people made long journeys on foot. The Bull, the **Drovers'** Arms, or the Herders' Inn tell us about groups of drovers whose job it was to walk their animals to market. These pubs are beside roads which were once wide and grassy. They became known as drovers' roads.

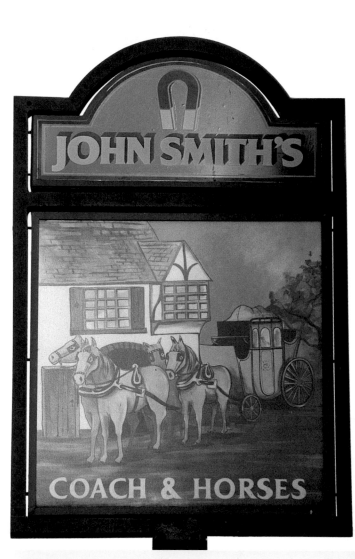

This sign is a reminder that this inn used to be a place where a stagecoach stopped to pick up passengers.

LOOK OUT

Can you find any clues about the work people did in the past in the place where you live? Do people still do this work today?

Burnley: a town

Burnley and Colyton

Burnley is quite a large **town** in Lancashire, which is in the north of England. Colyton is a **village** in the south of England, in the county of Devon. These two places are quite different. You can discover what they are like now, what they were like in the past, and the reasons why they are different.

What is Burnley like?

Burnley is a town. On this page you will see an **aerial photograph** of the town centre of Burnley. If the photograph showed a wider view of the town you would see rows and rows of houses.

On the edge of the town you would see modern factories and supermarkets. Do you live in a town like Burnley? How is your place different?

Beginnings

Anglo-Saxons, who lived here over 1000 years ago, gave Burnley its name. It was a place beside a river crossing, and had a market and a church. If we could travel back 200 years we would see that Burnley was then a small country town. Many of its people wove woollen cloth on **looms** in their cottages, or worked in coal-mines.

This is a photograph of Burnley in 1992.
Look for the different ways people can choose to travel from Burnley.

Why did Burnley grow?

A **canal** was built through the town of Burnley in the 1790s. It joined Lancashire and Yorkshire towns to the port of Liverpool. Cotton from America was carried from Liverpool to Burnley on canal **barges**. Cotton **mills** were built beside the river. Water from the river was used to turn **water-wheels**, which **powered** the machinery in the mills. People moved to Burnley to work in the mills.

Steam power

At the beginning of Queen Victoria's reign, businessmen began to build steam-powered cotton mills beside the canal. Burnley was the right sort of place for steam engines. Coal was taken from the coal-mines in Burnley, and burned to make the steam in the new engines. The steam power made machinery in the mills work faster, so more cloth could be made. Soon Burnley was a smoky town, full of cotton mills and chimneys.

More people and more houses

The **Victorian** mill owners and coal-mine owners needed more workers. People moved to Burnley from country villages. Rows of houses were built for them and the town grew.

A railway was built in the 1840s. This speeded up transport to Liverpool. Cotton arrived more quickly which meant that more workers could do more work, and so the town continued to grow.

*The children are investigating their town to see if it has grown like Burnley. Jyoti is sorting photographs of road names and **pub** signs to work out what her town was like in Victorian times.*

Colyton: a village

What is Colyton like?

Colyton is a **village**. If you look at the photographs you will notice Colyton is a smaller place than Burnley and has fewer large buildings.

Colyton has about twenty shops, which is rather a lot for such a small place, and there are no supermarkets. There are restaurants and **pubs** and a few places for holiday visitors to stay. There are many farmers who live with their families in farm houses near the village.

Beginnings

Like Burnley, it was the **Anglo-Saxon** people who lived here and gave Colyton its name. It means the village by the River Coly. It was a place by a river crossing where there was a market and a church.

If we could travel back 200 years we would see that Colyton was very like Burnley at that time. The farmers kept sheep and many people wove woollen cloth in their cottages. Both places had a corn **mill** and a woollen mill for washing newly-made cloth. These mills were **powered** by **water-wheels**.

This photograph of Colyton was taken in 1996 from a hill behind the village.

Why is Colyton a small place?

When steam-powered machinery began to be used to make cloth, Burnley grew but Colyton did not. Steam-powered engines needed coal, which Burnley had under the ground. Colyton only had **chalk** under the ground. So no new steam-powered mills were built in Colyton. Also, it was not worth building a **canal** because there were no heavy loads to transport.

Steam-powered mills in other places could make better cloth more quickly than in Colyton. Not enough people wanted to buy cloth made by the **hand-loom weavers** in Colyton. Many of the people of Colyton had no work.

Changes

In the 1820s, 1830s and 1840s some people left Colyton to look for work in London or other **towns** and cities. Some went to towns like Burnley to find work in the cotton or woollen mills. Colyton became even smaller. But some people stayed there.

They found other work. Women and children worked at home. They made **lace** and sold it for a little money. Paper was made at the water mill.

Steam trains come to Colyton

In the 1860s a railway was built and the Colyton farmers decided to keep cows instead of sheep. They could send the milk in churns by train to London and earn more money. Women and girls from the village worked on the farms milking cows and making cheese and butter. But there were still very few jobs for men.

Rebecca and Mark are sorting out names of places in Colyton. They want to find out what the village is like, and what the people do there.

In **Victorian** times there were no good reasons for people to move to Colyton, so the village did not grow.

Colyton today

Some people work in the village. There is a factory that makes chairs in one of the old water mills and a modern factory which makes parts for electrical plugs. These factories are not large.

Some people choose to live in the village although they work in other places. Their children go to Colyton Primary School. Do you live in a village like Colyton? How is your place different?

Glossary

aerial photograph a photograph taken from the air. The photograph of the land below might be taken from an aeroplane or hot-air balloon.

Anglo-Saxon people who came from Europe to live in Britain, over 1000 years ago

barge a boat that travels on canals, and was often used to carry cargo

blacksmith a person who makes things out of iron, and puts horse-shoes on horses

brickmaker a person who makes the bricks used in buildings

canal a channel of water which has been built for boats to travel along

cargo food and goods carried by a ship from one place to another; bananas, cars, cotton, and sugar are examples

carriage a four-wheeled cart, pulled along by a horse

chalk a soft, white rock found underground

coat of arms a shield painted with the badge of a wealthy family. The badge has a special design which was chosen to tell people something about the family.

collier a coal-miner

coronation a ceremony when the crown is placed on a new king's or queen's head for the first time. People celebrate this special day.

datestone a carved stone built into the wall of a house which records the year the house was built

diamond jubilee a celebration of 60 years; people celebrated the 60th year of Queen Victoria's reign in 1897

drover a person whose job it was to walk animals from farms to markets far away. Drovers walked their animals along wide grassy roads called droves.

ford a place in a river where it is possible for people or animals to walk through the water and cross from one side to the other

glassblower a person who blows down tubes into balls of hot, liquid glass to make glass shapes like bottles, glasses and patterns in window panes

hand loom a simple loom with no power, worked by a weaver's hands

industrial a place where things are made by machinery in factories

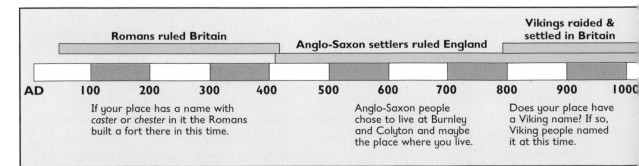

									Vikings raided & settled in Britain
	Romans ruled Britain				Anglo-Saxon settlers ruled England				

AD   100   200   300   400   500   600   700   800   900   1000

If your place has a name with *caster* or *chester* in it the Romans built a fort there in this time.

Anglo-Saxon people chose to live at Burnley and Colyton and maybe the place where you live.

Does your place have a Viking name? If so, Viking people named it at this time.

inn a place where people can stay overnight, and have something to eat and drink

landscape an area of land; it can be covered by grass, hills, mountains or buildings

lace threads woven to make pretty patterns

looms machines for weaving cloth. At first they were worked by the force of people's hands, arms and legs; later they used water power, steam power or electricity.

mills a type of factory where work is done with machinery

moored ships and boats that have been tied with ropes to the land

powered the way in which parts of machinery are made to work

pub a place where people can drink and eat. Some pubs also have rooms where people can stay overnight.

quarry a place where stone is dug out of the ground

quarryman a man who cuts stones from rock under the ground. The stones are used for building.

Roman a person or time when the Roman Empire ruled over Britain and a lot of other places

roper a person who makes ropes

time-line a line of things or people which have been put into order, with the oldest at one end and the newest at the other

town a place where there are lots of buildings and many people live

valley a long piece of land with sloping sides. There is often a river running along the bottom.

Victorian a person or thing which comes from the time when Queen Victoria was queen

Viking a person who came to Britain from across the sea about 1100 years ago

village a small group of houses with other buildings and farms

water-wheel a wheel that is pushed round by flowing water. As the wheel turns its pushing force makes machines work.

weaver a person who weaves threads together on a loom

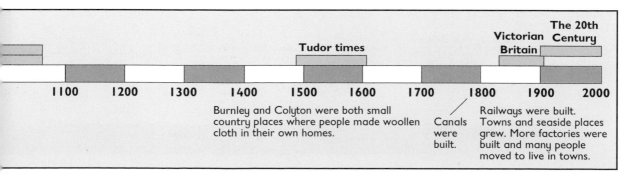

Tudor times

Victorian Britain

The 20th Century

1100 1200 1300 1400 1500 1600 1700 1800 1900 2000

Burnley and Colyton were both small country places where people made woollen cloth in their own homes.

Canals were built.

Railways were built. Towns and seaside places grew. More factories were built and many people moved to live in towns.

Index

Numbers in plain type (27) refer to the text. Numbers in italic type (27) refer to a caption or a picture.